We hope you enjoy coloring this book.

Download some extra

free coloring patterns

and get news of upcoming books at

www.scribblepresscoloring.com/free-download

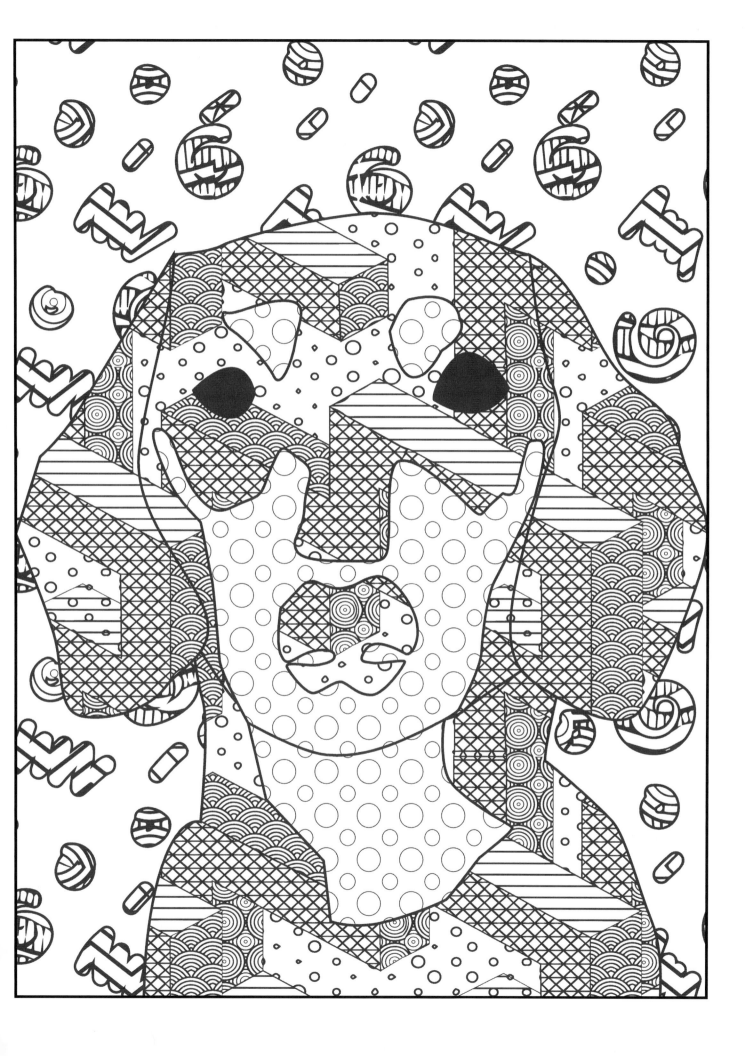

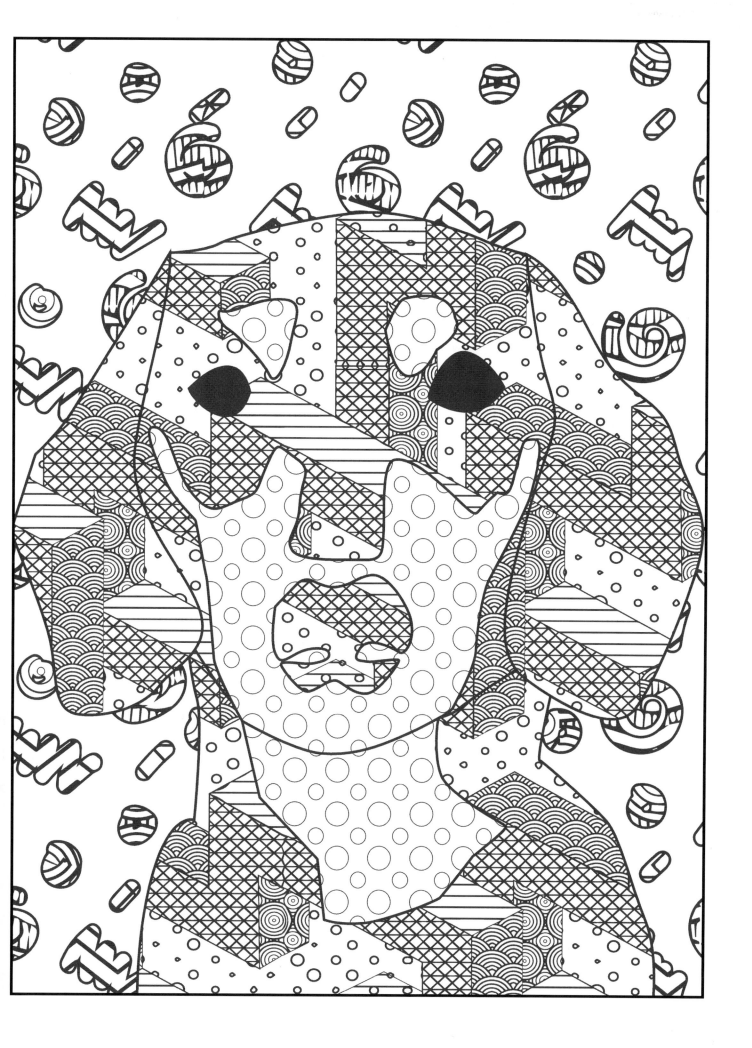

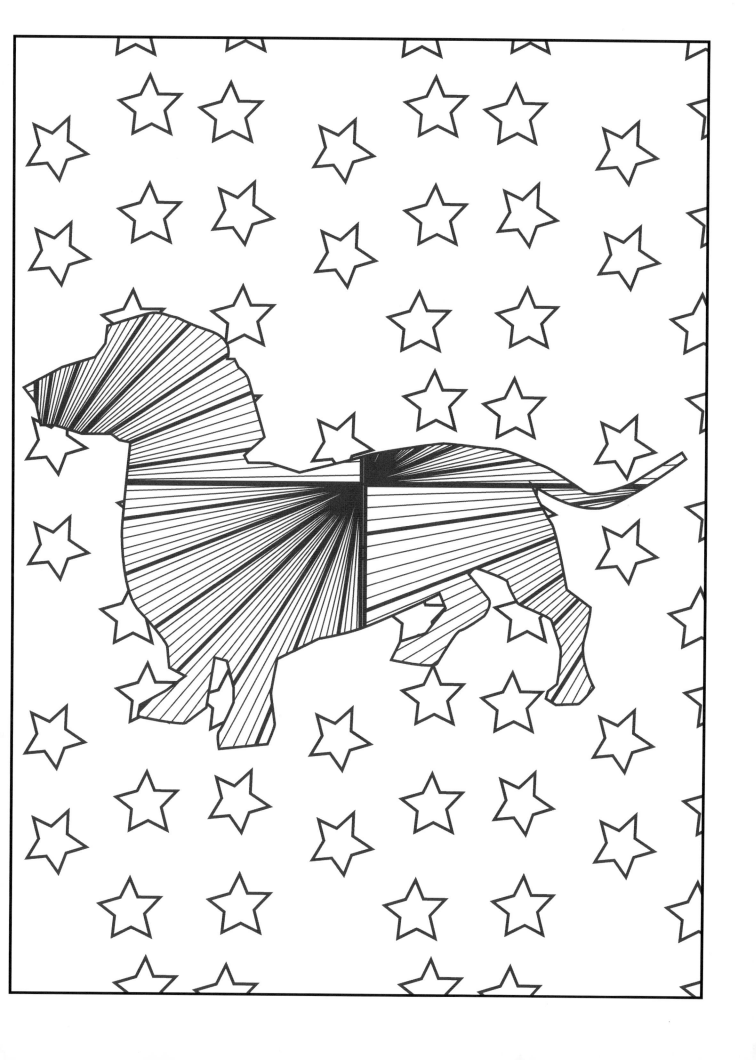

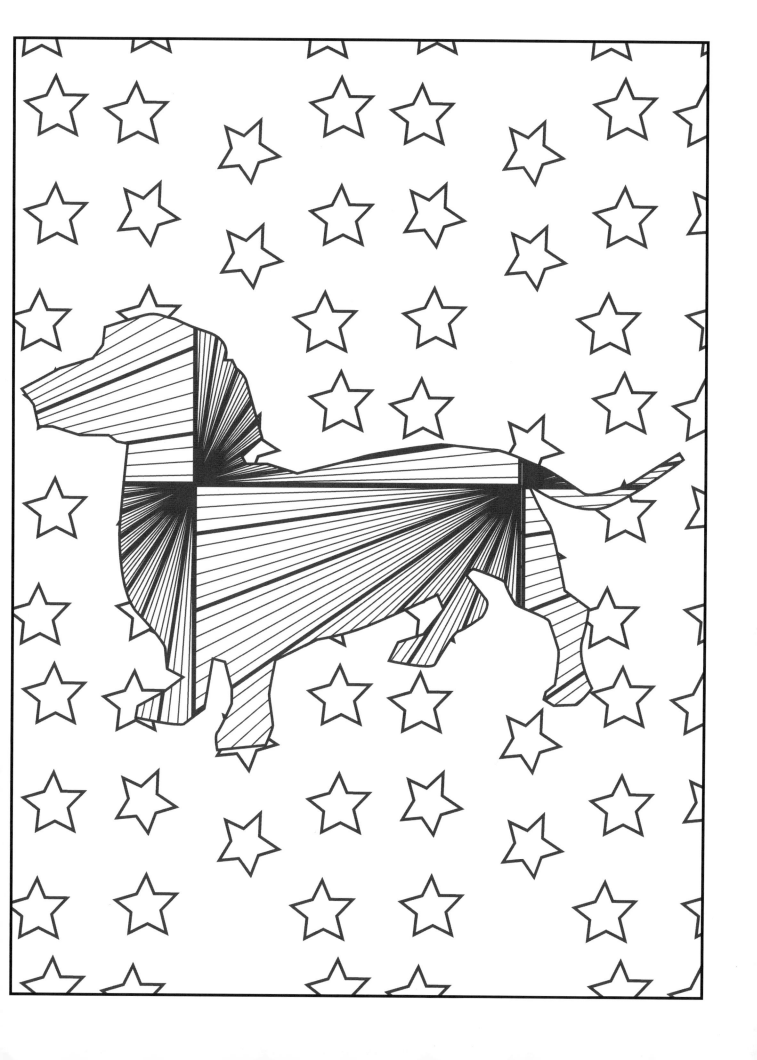

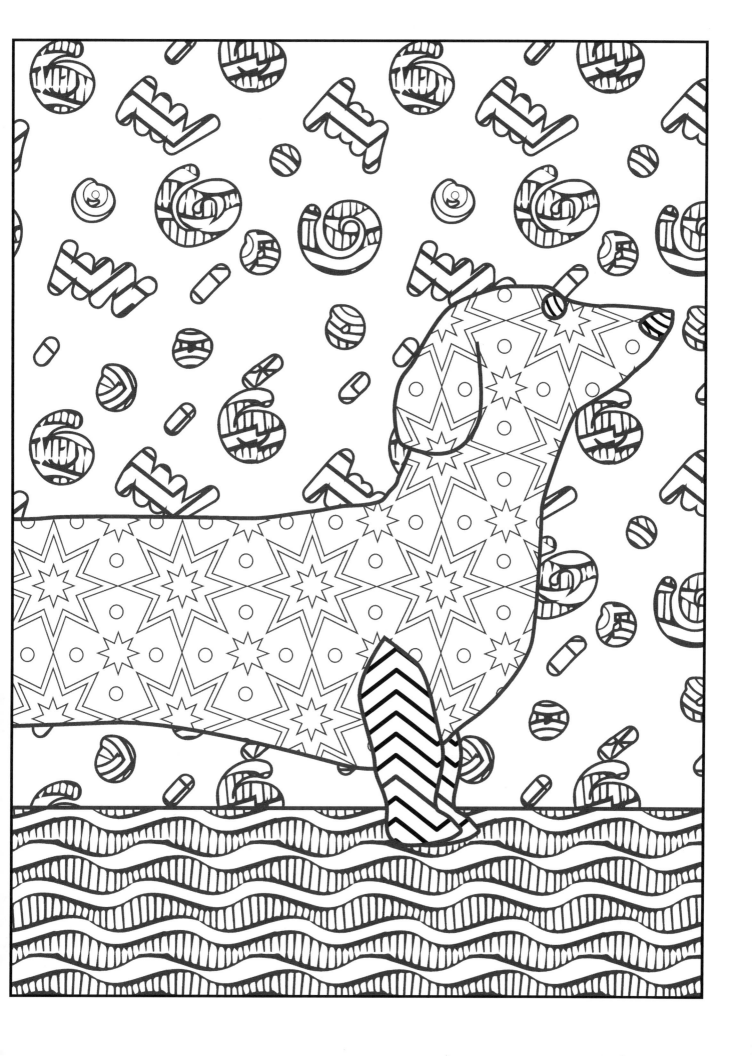

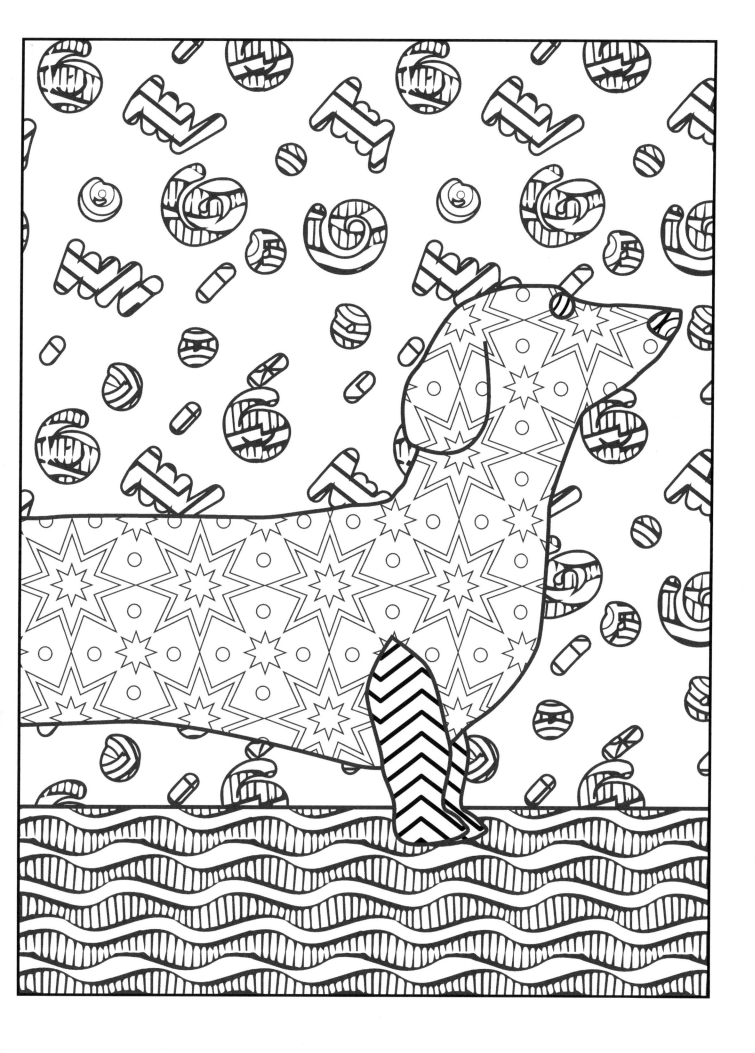

Made in the USA
Middletown, DE
14 December 2019